Write to Speak

© Copyright. All rights Reserved.

Teacher Manual

Dr. ET & COMPANY
LLC

TELPAS ready!

WRITE
to
SPEAK

Teacher Name_____

2023-2024

*Please make sure your students have access to individual Speaking and Writing TELPAS Levels for 2023

*Beginner
*Intermediate
*Advanced
*Advance High

dretandcompany.org

FIRST THINGS FIRST.

TOGETHER REVIEW IMPORTANT INFORMATION.

dretandcompany.org

#1
Being bilingual is a SUPERPOWER!

ADVANTAGES:

- Bilingualism is an asset
- Strong communication skills
- Decision making skills
- Memory advantage
- Language awareness

#2

The Power of COGNATES

Cognates are words that sound the same, and also have a similar meaning in different languages. Cognates also have some of the same words. Latin based words share many cognates.

There are 3 types of cognates:

*The words are spelled exactly the same

*The words are spelled almost the same, with a few differences

*The words are spelled differently, but sound the same

Here are some basic examples:

English Word	Spanish Word	German Word
Chocolate	chocolate	Schokolade
Mathematics	matemáticas	Mathematik
Social-Studies	estudios sociales	Sozialwissenschaften

dretandcompany.org

#3

ACADEMIC WORDS

Academic vocabulary, also known as academic words, are words that are used in all subjects. These words are specific to a content. Many academic words contain cognates from many languages.

When you write and speak make sure you are using academic vocabulary. Those are the words that you learn in all of your classes.

I like to call them "FANCY WORDS".
Share with students the list of academic words. Encourage them to find more and write them in.

Math Vocabulary Words

Use some of these words.	Write your own words here.
define	
duplicate	
identity	
observe	
recognize	
calculations	
describe	
demonstrate	
illustrate	
analyze	
question	
compare	
verify	
evaluate	
formulate	
translate	
parallel	
horizontal	
classify	
perimeter	
shapes (square, triangle, etc.)	
formula	
estimate	
sphere	

dretandcompany.org

Science

Use some of these words.	Write your own words here.
hypothesis experiment cells category weather human being oxygen living organism matter mass Five senses energy (types of energy) fossil electricity bacteria scientific hygiene H20 photosynthesis carbon monoxide carbon dioxide radiation diabetes	

dretandcompany.org

Social Studies/History

Use some of these words.	Write your own words here.
invention time creation government community city country state geography continent ancient times oceans economy geography citizen religion war battle communism elections republican democrat descendants kingdom liberty freedom Industry Political Constitution	

dretandcompany.org

#4

Idioms

An idiom is an expression that presents a figurative, non-literal meaning.

Idiom	Meaning
Once in a blue moon.	Rarely happens.
Through thick and thin.	No matter how difficult it is.
Sat on the fence.	Can't make a decision.
My heart is in the right place.	I have good intentions.
It cost an arm and a leg.	It was very expensive.
Spill the tea.	Give me the gossip.
Under the weather.	Feeling sick or sad.
When pigs fly.	It will never happen.
A blessing in disguise.	Something bad turns good.
A piece of cake.	Something that's easy.
Let the cat out of the bag.	Accidentally revealing a secret.
Break a leg.	Good luck.
The last straw.	Lost complete patience.
Bite the bullet.	Doing something unpleasant.

dretandcompany.org

#5

This is NOT a normal exam. Think of playing a computer game. It is all about strategy and beating the obstacles in order to reach the next level. Students are required to speak in a way that is a bit outrageous and exaggerated.

In order to achieve the highest scores you must.......

Speak using advanced academic words.
Speak for at least 50 seconds.
Speak clearly and loudly.

What is the most successful way to reach this requirement?

Write.
Proofread.
Read all of your sentences back loudly and clearly while you record.

Let's practice!

In other words, if we answer like "normal" people, our sentences will not be enough. Allow me to explain....

dretandcompany.org

What do you see here?

My normal response would be "clouds". However, this would not be an advanced high response.

An advanced high response would include academic words that are appropriate to the grade level. An advanced high response could be something like this:

"I observe different types of clouds. My favorite are the cumulonimbus clouds. It is apparent that this is a beautiful summer day in Northern California. The winds are blowing 25 miles per hour during the evening hours."

dretandcompany.org

Let's Practice. Look at the picture. Next, come up with two sentences per subject about the picture. You can describe it, create a narrative about what you see, or use your imagination. Make sure you use academic vocabulary.

1. What do you see in this photo that connects to Math? Science? Social Studies?
2. The last square can be anything of your choice. What do you see in this photo that pertains to your lived experience, your own life, a sport, class assignment, a reading activity? This is the "option" square.

Here are some examples. Check out the academic words which are highlighted.

MATH	SCIENCE
The two people are carrying a basket that weighs 70 pounds. **I see a brown basket made of 100 pieces of wood.**	**Two living organisms are walking with a basket made of recycled material.** **Apples are great fruit to eat for the digestive system.**
SOCIAL STUDIES	YOUR CHOICE
North America is a place where you can find apples. **Apples are transported from all over the continent.**	**I don't like to consume apples; they are not good for my digestive system.** **Playing technology games is more fun than picking apples.**

dretandcompany.org

REMIND STUDENTS TO INCLUDE:

ACADEMIC WORDS
(Synonyms, "fancy" words)

MATH

SCIENCE

SOCIAL STUDIES

OPTIONAL

dretandcompany.org

M.S.S.O. QUADRANT

Math	Science
Social Studies	**Optional**

***Proofread. Read and record.

dretandcompany.org

M.S.S.O. QUADRANT

Math	Science
Social Studies	Optional

****Proofread. Read and record.

dretandcompany.org

M.S.S.O. QUADRANT

Math	Science
Social Studies	**Optional**

***Proofread. Read and record.

M.S.S.O. QUADRANT

Math	Science
Social Studies	**Optional**

***Proofread. Read and record.

dretandcompany.org

M.S.S.O. QUADRANT

Math	Science
Social Studies	Optional

***Proofread. Read and record.

dretandcompany.org

19

M.S.S.O. QUADRANT

Math	Science
Social Studies	**Optional**

***Proofread. Read and record.

M.S.S.O. QUADRANT

Math	Science
Social Studies	Optional

***Proofread. Read and record.

dretandcompany.org

M.S.S.O. QUADRANT

Math	Science

Social Studies	Optional

***Proofread. Read and record.

dretandcompany.org

M.S.S.O. QUADRANT

Math	Science

Social Studies	Optional

***Proofread. Read and record.

dretandcompany.org

M.S.S.O. QUADRANT

Math	Science

Social Studies	Optional

***Proofread. Read your response.

dretandcompany.org

M.S.S.O. QUADRANT

Math	Science
Social Studies	Optional

***Proofread. Read and record.

dretandcompany.org

M.S.S.O. QUADRANT

Math	Science
Social Studies	**Optional**

***Proofread. Read and record.

dretandcompany.org

M.S.S.O. QUADRANT

Math	Science

Social Studies	Optional

***Proofread. Read and record.

dretandcompany.org

M.S.S.O. QUADRANT

Math	Science

Social Studies	Optional

***Proofread. Read and record.

dretandcompany.org

M.S.S.O. QUADRANT

Math	Science
Social Studies	**Optional**

***Proofread. Read and record.

dretandcompany.org

M.S.S.O. QUADRANT

Math	Science
Social Studies	Optional

***Proofread. Read and record.

dretandcompany.org

Compare / Contrast Similarities? Differences?

Look at the two pictures.

- What is the same?
- What is different?
- Compare them.

Fact / Opinion

➢ A fact is something that can be proven and true.
➢ An opinion is a judgment or thought about something that is not based on facts.

Math		Science	
Photo 1	Photo 2	Photo 1	Photo 2

Social Studies		Fact or Opinion	
Photo 1	Photo 2	Photo 1	Photo 2

Here are extra photos for practice. Create your own M.O.S.S. Quadrant.
Check off the ones you have completed.

○

○

dretandcompany.org

Here are more photos for practice. Create your own M.O.S.S. Quadrant.
Check off the ones you have completed.

○

○

dretandcompany.org

Here are photos for practice. Create your own M.O.S.S. Quadrant.
Check off the ones you have completed.

○

○

dretandcompany.org

Here are photos for practice. Create your own M.O.S.S. Quadrant.
Check off the ones you have completed.

○

○

dretandcompany.org

Compare & Contrast Photos

dretandcompany.org

It is GO TIME!

PROOFREAD FIRST. THEN READ/RECORD.

DO NOT PAUSE OR STOP

SPEAK LOUDLY

IF YOU LOSE YOUR SPOT, START AGAIN. SKIP WORDS YOU CAN'T READ

READ LIKE A BOSS 50 Seconds! Or more!

dretandcompany.org

MY NOTES

dretandcompany.org

Bilingualism is a SUPERPOWER!

@dretontheborder

dretandcompany.org